Real World Wedding

Planning Your Dream Wedding

Without

The Financial Nightmare

Kristen Hull

ISBN-10: 1499636830
ISBN-13: 9781499636833

Table of Contents

Introduction:

Congratulations! If you're reading this book then it's on – you're getting married and you have a wedding to plan! First of all, let me wish you all the best in your future married life. May life bless you and your spouse with a lifetime of love, good fortune and joy.

Now presumably, you're also reading this book because not only do you have a weeding to plan, but you need to do it on a budget. Perhaps you've been dreaming of this special day since you were a little girl, drawing pictures in your mind of the perfect fairytale wedding with all the bells and whistles: the elegant ballroom, the full band, silverware and glasses gleaming on tables laid out for a specially-catered sumptuous feast…the works. But now you face the harsh reality: you simply can't afford "the works." What now?

Planning for a wedding should be one of the most enjoyable and unforgettable times of your life, a time to make a lot of fun-packed, happy memories that will bring you joy throughout your life. Sadly, this isn't the case for many people. The wedding planning stage is associated with a lot of negativity and stress, especially when your budget is limited. Do images come to mind of those stressed out, near hysterical brides breaking down in tears because this or that can't be "just right" because it's simply too expensive?

Every bride to be (and even some grooms, though they won't be caught dead admitting it) wants that grand, sophisticated wedding that is the stuff of dreams. But what if you don't have a rich daddy to foot the bill? What if your family has offered to pay for the wedding but their budget is modest? Perhaps you and your fiancé are paying for it out of your own salaries or savings while still paying off college loans? Whatever the case, the big all-out wedding is out of the question.

> **Fun Fact: The 2006 wedding of Tom Cruise and Nicole Kidman held in a 15th century castle cost $2 million, making it one of the 10 most expensive weddings in the world.**

Knowing the average costs of a wedding may help you know where you stand. Statistics show that in the USA, the average wedding covering everything from bridal dress, catering, photography and band or DJ is in the range of $28,671. The cheapest has been recorded at $500 -$1000, although in my opinion that's rather a tight fit. Some of the most expensive weddings in the world range between 1 million and a whopping $75 million – which I again think is way over the top even if you can afford it, with so much needy people in the world. Some couples may resort to extreme methods such as borrowing money to selling their cars to splurge on luxurious, showy wedding – and I can guarantee you they have come to regret it.

Moderation is the key. Knowing where you stand financially, how much you can realistically afford to spend on your wedding will save you a lot of future grief. A dream wedding does not have to break the bank. It can be done on a budget without cutting too many corners. With a little research and imagination it can be done on a working man's salary – and you won't have to sell your car spend months paying off the bills. Remember this: Money can't buy style and elegance; that's up to your creativity and a little help from friends and family – just ask them and you will be amazed at how eagerly and selflessly they'll pitch in to help make your special day unique and memorable.

This book will walk you through the stages of planning an amazing wedding suited to your particular budget, allowing you to enjoy every moment of the planning process: choosing your gown, sending out the invitations, deciding on the flowers and much more. You will be stress-free, focused and calm throughout the planning stage up to your big day. You will discover some of the best tips and tricks from experts to cut costs without cutting on class and style. We'll explore various alternatives to saving money on everything that's on your list, from bridal dress to wedding photos and I can guarantee that your guests will be talking about your amazing, well-planned wedding for weeks to come.

Finally, planning a wedding may be a bit overwhelming for a first-time bride on a budget, even with a wedding planner. So I'm offering you a set of detailed checklists as a special giveaway with this book that will make your work that much easier. You can get them from my website:

http://www.realworldweddingplanning.com

Now read on and prepare to be amazed!

Where to Start?

"It is better to take many small steps in the right direction than to make a great leap forward only to stumble backward." Old Chinese proverb.

There's so much to do that just figuring out where to start can be nerve-wracking, more so if you don't have ample time. Ideally, it would be great if you had between 6 months to a year between the time he popes the question and the big day, but this is not the case with most weddings. With proper planning you can get everything done in two months and still have time for a last bachelorette party with your girlfriends the night before!

The wedding planner at the end of this book and the giveaway checklists provided will be invaluable to you – make them your bests friends. Your first step is to invest in a cheap notebook and a divider folder. The notebook is to jot down ideas and reminders, the folder is for your checklists, receipts and quotes.

The following steps will get you well on your way into the planning process:

Who pays?

Traditionally, it is the bride's parents who pay for the wedding but in reality that's not always the case. If your parents offer to pay for the wedding, great. Better yet, if your fiancé's parents offer to contribute then your budget's just gone up! Discuss it together and see if he feels comfortable about asking his parents to help out. Even a couple of thousand dollars extra can go a long way. Some future in-laws get together to discuss the wedding and who will pay what; if you can arrange that, do so as quickly as possible so you can proceed with the arrangements.

How much?

Whether it's your parents, future in-laws or you who will foot the bill, the next thing to be made clear is the budget. Write it in big, clear letters at the top of your notebook and make a promise to stick to it.

Just remember, costs can quickly run up if you're not careful and whoever's paying may not be happy about forking out the extra cash. If you can afford it, put aside a sum of your own money for any run-over or last minute expenses or extras that you simply feel you need to have.

Traditional is cheaper

I'm assuming that you will go for a traditional wedding instead of a theme event. Theme weddings general cost more; if you try to do them on a tight budget or cut corners they will simply come off as extremely tacky. For example, a Hawaiian theme with fake orchids and leis and your brother playing the ukulele will simply have guests roaring into their champagne glasses. If you can't have it in Hawaii don't have it. But that's just my personal opinion.

Time and place

So we're assuming you want a traditional wedding. The next step is to decide on the date and place of the wedding. This includes booking both the church and the reception hall.

The date is important and could be a big money-saver. Traditionally, most couples prefer to tie the knot on a Saturday. There's no specific reason for this but I suspect it's to facilitate things for relatives and guests flying or driving in from long distances, and for everyone to have recovered from the festivities by Monday morning. Obviously, Saturday wedding being so much in demand, they are also by far the most expensive as well.

Remember, getting creative is the key here. Why not tie the knot on a Tuesday or Wednesday? You can save quite a nice sum by planning your wedding on a normal weekday. You can be sure that your favorite aunt, best friend or any other special person in your life will find a way to be with you on your big day not matter what that day is. Another cheaper alternative is a bank holiday Sunday.

An added bonus to the cheaper rates is that you'll find more bookings on non-traditional dates. Also, many locations that offer to hold weddings offer discounts on an off day so you may want to consider that.

The time you hold your reception can also be a good money-saver. If you're on a really tight budget, sometime between noon and 5 p.m. (when your guests will already have had lunch) will of course spare you the expense of serving lunch and dinner. Some elegant finger foods and wedding cake should keep your guests satisfied until the reception is over.

The months between November and April are also good money savers. Not only are bookings cheaper but you can ask for an added discount for booking in the off-season.

Important points to consider when booking your wedding hall

The first decision to be made is where the service and the reception are to be held. Wedding and reception halls need to be reserved well in advance (at least 3 to 4 months before the wedding if possible) as most venues are sometimes fully booked for months in advance. Discuss with your spouse what type of venue would best reflect your style and uniqueness, i.e., whether the reception will be more on the formal side or whether you both prefer something casual and upbeat. This should help you narrow things down a bit.

Make a list of all the potential reception halls and hotels In the area and that you are considering and book an appointment to visit each one. I know, it's an exhausting, time consuming task but with the right mindset it can fun and challenging as well, and the right venue is a major factor in the success of your wedding. Check the unsuitable places off your list and narrow it down to two or three places, then make your decision.

> Tip: If your budget is really tight, consider having the reception in a private home. Perhaps you have a relative or friend with a spacious home and garden who would be happy to host your wedding party.

If you or a family member belong to a club or benevolent association you may want to add that to your list. Most places like these offer discounts to members as well as a much bigger garden or reception area and again, remember to book early.

In addition to the costs, remember to ask the right questions when booking to ensure that the venue and services provided suit your specific needs:

1- How many guests are coming? Make as close an estimate as you can of the number of guests you plan on inviting. as the reception hall must be large enough to accommodate everyone comfortably.
2- When visiting the venue, make a quick note of the dancing area and that it's not too cramped.
3- Be very clear from that start what you will get for your money, what extras you may need to pay for later or if there's anything you need to rent. For example, hotel ballroom packages usually cover everything from band, silverware, to catering and the wedding cake for a fixed fee. Other venues may require you to hire your own caterers or band.
4- What little "extras" does the venue offer? Some venues may provide little extras like plants, candles or centerpieces that save you hassle and money.

5- Does the venue provide ample parking space and is it free? Some venues offer valet which of course will makes things much smoother for your guests.

6- Some venues may also have their own officiants offer to hold both the ceremony and the reception which may be cheaper. If you prefer to be married by your own priest ask if outside officiants are allowed.

7- If there will be children, you may prefer to have a special eating area to be reserved for this. Ask if this can be accommodated.

8- When you visit, check for scenic areas that would make could spots for wedding pictures.

9- Are changing rooms available for the bridal party?

10- Ask if a deposit is required – in most cases, it is.

We'll learn more later on about making your dream reception a success but now that booking the venue has been checked off your list, it's time to plan the next step – the guest list!

"We invite you to share in the joy"… The invitation

Remember the dividing folder mentioned earlier? This is where you will organize a list of all the people that you and your spouse want to share your special day with. It's good etiquette to ask your parents and future un-laws to provide you with a list of the guests they would like to invite as well. Depending on the number of guests you have booked for, you may want to ask them to keep their lists to a specific number of invitees. If they know you're on a budget – and more so if they are paying for the wedding on a budget– you should have no objections.

A word of caution to you as well – you do not have to invite everyone you know. This is where you cut corners. If it's a small family affair people will understand and if not, nobody in your larger circle of acquaintances will be really offended so don't obsess too much about that. Believe it or not, people don't really like to go to weddings of people they don't know too well and actually find them quite tedious. Just drop the word at the office that you're planning a small wedding on a budget and your colleagues will understand. Unless they are people to talk to on a daily basis, they'll never notice or probably care if they're not invited.

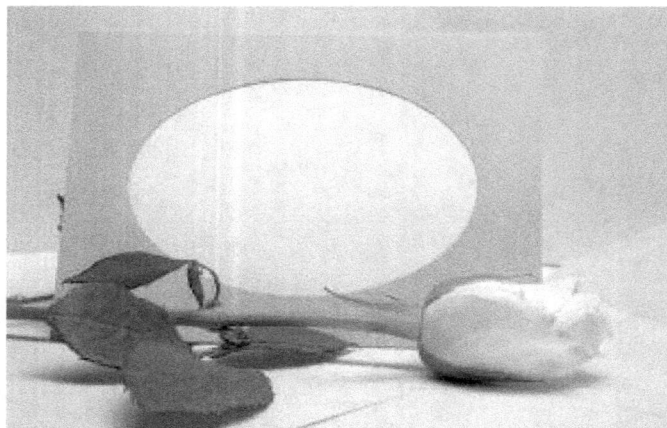

Ideally, invitations should be sent out 6 – 8 weeks before the big day to give guests enough time to make arrangements and RSVP, and give you enough time to replace any cancellations. Once you've settle on a guest list, you'll know how many invitations you'll need and you can move on to the next step – the design.

Wedding invitations should not be expensive nor should you waste too much time on them. You might pore over different designs for hours, imagining how this or that one in it's pretty envelope Elegant lettering will make an impression – and it will, but only for about a minute! The recipient will then read the contents, send an RSVP and toss it aside the invitation or throw it away. Just pick a nice, simple (and cheap) design out of a few samples and get the invitations out.

Do it yourself

Make a statement by making your own wedding invitations. Not only is this loads cheaper but it's fun, creative and the end result will be fantastic. Make it a fun-filled memorable event by inviting your girlfriends or bridesmaids over to help. They will love the idea - the more hands the better if your guest list is long! Here are some ideas:

- Create wedding invitations on your computer using Photoshop r even MS Word. If you're fiancé's into computers, this is one task he might enjoy doing with you.

- Make cards from cardstock in your favorite color or your wedding colors and get creative by decorating with bits of ribbon, lace or fake gemstones.

- Check out your local shops DYI packs that can end up being even cheaper.

- Look in the online for ideas. There are dozers of websites that offer designs, wording, and even step-by step instructions for making your own invitations. Just Google "Make your own wedding invitations."

- There are quite a few inexpensive software programs for specifically creating personalized invitations and greeting cards. I would recommend investing in one such program as it will make your task much less easier, and can be used over and over for many other occasions such as Christmas, birthday, anniversaries and much more.

- For a more professional look consider taking your designed card to a specialized copy shop. They can print out your cards on the paper of your choice.

Wording

What you choose to write in your invitation is another reflection of your uniqueness. Just make sure all the important information is included, included such time and place. Etiquette states that all words must be spelled out in full (For example, Wyoming instead of WY). It's not required to include middle names or the names of your parents. Use a legible font and double-check for any errors before printing out the cards.

Making your own wedding cards is a chance for you and your fiancé to set the tone for your wedding day, and the wording should reflect your vision of how you envisage that day will be. Don't get carried away, thought; one or two simple lines should say it all.

Make things easy for your guests by including a postcard (with stamp) along with the invitation for RSVP. All your guests have to do is fill it out and drop it in the mailbox, leaving less room for delay and forgetfulness.

If you're not keen on buying stamps for all those postcards if your guest list is long, you can print RSVP information at the bottom of your wedding invitation. Provide a phone number and email address

Envelopes

As you may have seen with wedding invitations you've received in the mail, the conventional route is for the invitation to be placed in a matching envelope and both placed in an outer envelope with the stamp and address.

This is not carved in stone and will definitely up your costs. Placing the invitation alone in the mailing envelope will not raise any eyebrows and is perfectly fine.

The most efficient way to address envelopes is with labels printed out on your (I recommend clear labels as they just look better). Avery labels is an awesome website that offers a wide variety of label templates so you might want to check that out here: www.Quill.com/**Avery**-Label-Makers

If you prefer a more personal touch then go ahead and address the envelopes by hand but if you have really horrendous handwriting, please be honest with yourself and consider another option! Just note that this is a pretty time consuming task if your guest list is long, so it's best delegated to one or two of your bridesmaids who have the nicest handwriting. You may want to check out some calligraphy tips online if you have the luxury of time. However, my best advice is to not spend too long nit-picking on the envelopes and move on to the next step.

Note: If your heart is absolutely set on having custom-made invitations, they will definitely cost you more than DIY but there are still some affordable choices that won't strain your budget too much. Check online for the best discounts.

You might have a friend or acquaintance who works in the business and can get you a discount. Another great option is to ask a friend or relative to pay for the invitations as an early wedding gift!

Finally - the biggest cost with regards to invitations is going to be the postage. There's no way you can get around this as post offices don't offer discounts on bulk mail!

Again it's time to get creative: arrange a day with your fiancé to personally deliver invitations to people living in your local area. You will be amazed at how touched and appreciative they will that you have personally taken the time to invite them in person – they will never guess the real reason!

Something old, something new... Attire

Your bridal attire

The wedding march start to play announcing the entrance of the bride. The guests turn expectantly, the groom stands up straighter. And there you are... a fairy, a sylph almost floating on a cloud of light, bathed in a radiant glow. Everyone gasps at your beauty... and at your absolutely breathtaking wedding gown...

How many of us have relived this scene in or fantasies? I would say almost every woman on the planet. .Now the time has come for you to live that moment for real ad your wedding attire is a very big part of it.

Choosing a wedding dress can be the most daunting of all the tasks a busy bride to be has to do but with the advice you'll read here it will hopefully be smooth sailing all the way. You don't need a custom-made, hand-embroidered dress that costs a month's rent. you can be every bit as elegant and stylish as in your girlhood fantasy on a budget with a little bit of planning creativity.

The very first thing you need to do is sit down with a sheet of paper and a pencil. Divide the paper into two columns. In the first column, list what you are absolutely certain that you want regarding the style of your dress. For example: white, long train, embroidery, scooped neck, lace sleeves, etc. In the second column list what you absolutely do not want: sleeveless, high waist, sequins, diamante trim, etc. Laying down the basics in this way will save you so much time and stress. And you should really should have a broad idea of what you want and do not want based on your own personal style and figure. Of course, if you're open to anything then you can skip this step.

Something old…

In many families, it's actually the tradition for brides to wear wedding gowns handed down from their mothers or grandmothers.

Assuming your mother or grandmother still own their dresses and they are in good condition, ask to wear them on your special day. The gesture will touch their hearts; imagine the ride on their faces when they see you walking down the aisle in the same dress they wore on their wedding day!

You will be pleasantly surprised as nothing really beats those classic styles and fabrics. However, if the style is outdated you can get a seamstress to make a few alterations here and there for as little as $100. Give it a good fry cleaning and you're set to go.

Why not opt for a second hand gown? I know that any brides find this cringe-worthy but a budget is a budget and let me tell you from experience that there are a lot of amazing finds for less than a quarter of the price of a brand new dress.

I've known bride's who've found absolute gems in thrift shops and consignment stores that won rave reviews from everyone who saw them. Check out eBay for some great discounts as well. Again, if alterations are needed it will only be a fraction of the cost.

Something new...

Bridal shops are exorbitantly expensive but how about a brand new dress from department store? Check you your local stores around prom season. You'll be surprised at the stunning styles, quality and cheap prices. Many shops will also run special offers on prom dresses to up sales during prom season.

Off the rack evening gowns and cocktail dresses can also be altered and embellished to transform into eye-opening wedding dresses.

This may be a bit far-fetched but check your local listings for going out of business sales at bridal shops. If you happen to get lucky, I know of people who have bought $1000 gowns for just $100 merely because the store was closing its doors!

The classifieds are an excellent place to shop for cheap wedding dresses. Some of these dresses have actually never been worn due to wedding not taking place. Some people may take this as a bad omen but if this doesn't make you uncomfortable you can really find some great bargains.

End of the season sales also offer an opportunity for some good bargain hunting, so check out your local mall.

Something copied...

Look through bridal catalogues for your dream gown and have a seamstress copy. The design. The pros: you will have the gown of your dreams without having to fork out loads of money. The cons: It will still be much more expensive than the other options listed here, especially if it involves a lot of delicate work. If your budget allows for this, great!

Remember that our motto is to be creative – do you know someone who's talented at sewing? Do you sew yourself? If so, you can pick out the fabric and accessories and make a dress that is totally your own for almost nothing!

Something "borrowed…"

Renting a wedding gown has become extremely popular these days for the practical bride on a budget. With so many advances in video and photography, it's no longer a must to buy a gown and keep it for sentimental purposes. Did you know that you can rent a dress with a retail value of $3000 for $75? That's why renting is the preferred choice of most brides today.

Veil, shoes and accessories

As long as you don't fall for the exaggerated prices at bridal shops, the bridal is up to your personal preference. Whether you prefer the traditional sheer veil covering your face, a delicately puffed cloud surrounding your heat or a more con-conventional headdress, it's all up to you. As long as you don't spend what you saved on your gown buying it!

A simple crown of flowers in your hair can also replace the traditional veil and be much cheaper as well. A spray of baby's breath for example is elegant, simple and will give you the appearance of a Greek goddess.

Did you know that you can buy tulle for as cheap as $1.99 a yard? Follow the instructions below to make your own stunning veil that will perfectly complement your dream gown.

What you will need:

- A base: this can be an inexpensive tiara, wire for the frame or hair combs to hold the veil in place. (Just remember that the veil should not overshadow your gown so if you have a lot going on in the dress, perhaps a tiara might be too much.)

- Glue gun.

- Embellishments of your choice (baby's breath, ribbons, bows, fake gemstones)

Bunch up the end of the tulle and glue it to your base. If it's a tiara, just glue directly to the base. For combs, make a "halo" of the tulle and glue the combs on either side to attach to your head.

Add your trimmings and voila – your veil is made!

Note: If you need more visual instructions I recommend YouTube. You will find many videos that will walk you through the process.

Shoes and accessories are the fun part. The best cost-saving tip here is to invest in shoes that can be worn later on with normal clothes or other evenings out.

Shoe shopping can be overwhelming due to the countless styles and colours available. Before you go shopping, decide on the basic style and color you're looking for and the stores you will shop at. Browsing online is also a good option. I have found numerous websites offering low-budget wedding shoes and some of them look really great.

Tips for buying shoes

- Take into consideration the season. Open toed shoes or flimsy sandals may not really be appropriate for wintertime.
- If you are wearing satin shoes, and getting married outdoors or in rainy season, apply a resistant spray to protect them.

- Ideally, your shoes should attach the color of your dress. If you can, bring a piece of your dress fabric with you or a close-up photo of your dress.
- Remember that you are going to be wearing your shoes and perhaps dancing in them for hours. Do not put style before comfort or you'll regret it, believe. A good balance between chic and comfort is the way to go. Walk around a bit when you try them on, and maybe perform a few dance steps to make sure the shoes fit you well and that you can move around easily in them.

Hair and makeup

Taking the whole bridal party to a hairdressing shop for makeup and hair can be pretty expensive. Simply arrange to all get together and do your makeup yourselves or call on friends or family for help. It shouldn't be too hard to find someone to help; a friend of a friend's who's a hairdresser, a cousin who's always been good at doing hair and makeup, or someone who will actually pay for the whole party to go to a professional salon – as an early wedding gift.

A note on makeup: Natural is always the way to go for a bride. The last thing you want to do is pile on makeup that upstages your bridal gown and makes you look unnatural and clownish.

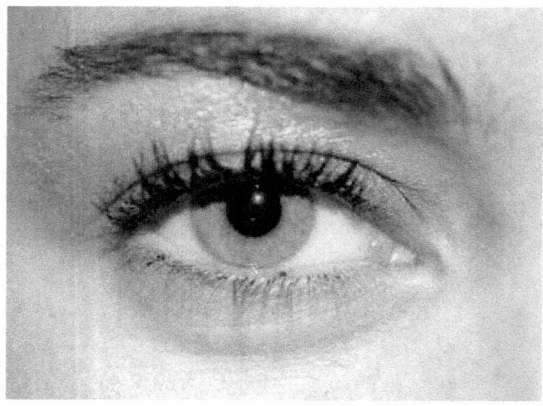

Your guests and your husband to be don't want to see someone they don't recognize walking down the aisle. They should be stunned by your overall look, not shocked by the layers of makeup on your face. So whatever you do – do not "experiment" with a new like on this of all days. Do not cake on foundation and eye shadow. Keep everything light to bring out your best features.

I recommend you and your bridesmaids have a "rehearsal makeup night" where you all get together and experiment with several looks and exchange opinions. It's fun and it will save you a lot of time on the big day.

Now that you're all suited out for your big day, what will your groom wear?

Bridal attire for the dashing groom

We all know the brides love picking out their wedding attire but that may not always hold true for the groom – so you may have to point him in the right direction here to make sure he doesn't leave things till the last minute, or picks something totally unsuitable.

What your groom wears will complete the picture of style and elegance and compliment your own bridal attire.

Tux or Suit?

The groom should choose his attire according to the formality of the wedding. For a semi-formal or formal wedding the groom will have to wear a tuxedo.

First of all, it's important that you know what the key differences are between a tuxedo and a suit. The biggest difference is that a tuxedo has satin in it, while a suit does not; the most popular colors are black, white and grey. He should consider darker colors for a fall or winter wedding and lighter colors for a spring or summer wedding.

If your groom decides on a tuxedo, then the cheapest and easiest way to get one is simply to rent it. Check your local outlets for the best prices. You may even get a discount for a mass rental (i.e., the best man, the groomsmen, your dad and father-in-law, etc.)

Is it inappropriate for the groom to wear a suit to the wedding? Definitely not, according to today's fashion trends! And in this case an even cheaper option is for him to wear a suit he already owns, perhaps one that he bought for a special occasion and hasn't worn since.

Your groom can also by his suit or tuxedo second hand and some stores offer great sales to help create dream weddings on limited budgets. As a matter of fact, it's likely that he'll find a suit or tuxedo at less than a rental price at these stores and he can resell or keep to wear on other occasions.

Something borrowed… for the groom!

Accessories are the key to bringing his suit to life and adding a touch of panache and flair. Consider the options of cufflinks, a pocket handkerchief, belt, tie-pin, or a watch. The best part is that all of these can be easily borrowed off buddies or relatives who will be more than happy to contribute to his special day. These little touches will give enhance your groom's unique style and complement your elegance as well.

Groomsmen and Bridesmaids

Groomsmen and bridesmaids usually rent their formal wear and this is by far the cheapest option for you. It's recommended that they rent their attire a month or two prior to the wedding. Check for shops in your area offering discounts if your wedding is in low season – or even ask for a discount.

The best thing to do on renting groomsmen attire is to go to a local tuxedo shop on the recommendation of a trusted friend or a family member. Some bridal shops carry groomsmen attire as well, so you might get a good bargain if you buy or rent your gown, as well as the whole bridal party's attire from the same store. I recommend you look into this option. It's a big time-saver and also a money-saver for everyone concerned, especially if groomsmen and bridesmaids are expected to pay for their own wedding attire.

Tip: You and your bridesmaids should all come to an agreement on what they will wear, the color, style and even if they should all wear their hair a certain way. How many times have we seen wedding videos where bridesmaids followed the bride with shoulders hunched, heads down, barely able to crack a smile? That's because they were uncomfortable with what they were wearing! They were forced into those tacky dresses by the bride and they're not happy about it.

So bear in mind to take all of your bridesmaids' preference into account. Choose a simple, upbeat style that looks good on everyone and a color that everyone likes. The last thing you want is your bridesmaids moping around miserably because they're unhappy with their look. A happy bridesmaid makes for a happy wedding!

Flowers

A bride's choice of flowers or arrangements reflects her taste and personality; they also provide the perfect finishing touch to the special day. Flowers include your bridal bouquet, flower arrangements at the church and reception hall and centerpieces.

There are no wrong or right choices when selecting flowers, it's a personal choice which has to work well with your budget. A good florist can provide helpful advice while sharing your vision – and helping you stay within your allotted budget.

The first step is to determine your budget. Bearing in mind that all flowers are beautiful whether cheap or expensive, you shouldn't really spend too much in this area. The following tips should help:

- Mix and match flower types to create unique arrangements that reflect the style of your wedding.
- Consider the color of your flowers, they do not necessarily have to match your gown but they shouldn't completely clash with it either.
- A good cost-cutting option is to choose seasonal flowers as they will be cheaper.
- Contact a local farmer rather than a florist for an even lower price - or consider picking them from your own garden if you have one.
- You can also use silk flowers if you want to save money, but take care; they're not always less expensive than fresh flowers.

Make your own flower arrangements and bridal bouquet

If you look see a beautiful bridal bouquet or flower arrangement online in a magazine or online that you fall in love with, why not consider making your own?

For your bridal bouquet, our good buddy YouTube will again come in handy here – there are loads of tip-packed videos that will walk you through the process way better than I can here, so check them out. Select a bouquet from a magazine or online, decide on the color and types of flowers and prepare to enjoy every minute.

Making your own flower arrangements for the church and reception hall can be cheap and easy if you follow these tips:

-   Select flowers that are in season.
-   Decide on a cool place for storage if you're planning to use fresh flowers as you will probably buy and start preparing them several days ahead of the big event. A good choice is to keep them in a mildly air-conditioned room don't let the cold air blow directly on the flowers.
-   Prepare a spacious working area to prepare your wedding flowers. A big kitchen area would be great or even outdoors, as you should keep the flowers in big buckets.
-   Be flexible, don't get hooked on a particular type of flower as long as the color and style fit your wedding theme.
-   Bear in mind that flowers may cost more during certain months (Like February when there are less flowers in season and they are more expensive due to Valentine's Day.) You may then want to consider artificial flowers.

How to:

-   You will need floral shears, bouquet pins, floral wrap of your choice and any embellishments you would like to add such as glitter, bow, bits of lace, etc.
-   **Set up your working area, keeping all flowers in big buckets.**
-   Prepare your flowers by snipping the stems to make sure they are all the same. length
-   Choose 2-4 flowers as an anchor to start the base of the bouquet bunch the stems together and bind them with floral tape.
-   Add more flowers around the anchored flowers while mixing textures and colors and continuously wrap the arrangement with floral tape as you're adding flowers.
-   When you reach the size you like, use a final wrap of your choice and finally pin the ribbon with the bouquet pins.

These arrangements can then be fastened to church pews or throughout the reception hall.

Finally, if you do have your heart set on a certain look that you are unable to achieve yourself, the only way is to order on line or from a local florist, and offer to provide the labor and/or materials yourself for a discount.

Flowers for your bridesmaids

Bridesmaids bouquets should really be DIY affairs and not too costly or time consuming.. Choose the flowers in season then the color that matches with the wedding theme. You can add little finishing touches that look great such as ribbon, lace, or even decorative wire to hold all the flowers together, you can also add a pin to give the bouquet a charming look.

NOTE: The bridesmaid bouquet should smaller than the bride's bouquet; it also must contain at least one of the flowers in the bride's bouquet.

If you are using fresh flowers, make sure they remain as fresh as possible for as long as possible. Ideally, you should make the bouquets the night before the wedding and keep them in a cool room. This is an good task to delegate to your bridesmaids.

As for boutonnieres, they should be as simple as possible as they will be worn by the men. To make a boutonniere, take a simple flower and add to it a few green leaves, and just wrap the stem in floral tape, and that's it!

If your bridesmaids will be wearing corsages instead of carrying bouquets, you can use the same method for making boutonniere but with 3-5 flowers. Gather the flowers together and wrap around the stems with floral tape which comes in green and white, and add accessories if desired

Having a flower girl will not be an extra cost and will be a sweet addition to your wedding. A cute and eagerly willing child is easy to find, little baskets cost next to nothing and you already have the flowers!

For the flower girl basket, you should consider the age and size of the flower girl before buying it then decide whether you want it filled with arranged flowers with petals that will be scattered – or both if you prefer.

Check with your church first, as some have restrictions against using fresh flower petals in and in this case you can buy silk flower petals.

What's the theme? Decorating the wedding venue

The church

When decorating a church for a wedding there are a few things to keep in mind, first of all you have to talk to the person in charge at the church to make sure certain decorations are allowed. Some churches don't allow you to decorate the altar, for examples. When thinking decorations, think candles and ribbons; one because they're cheap and two, they are very easy to clean up. Candles can often be more romantic but just make sure to put them in enclosed things like cylinders or fireproof bags so that nothing can catch on fire.

Twinkle lights are also inexpensive and the really tiny ones make perfect church decorations because they look like small, twinkling stars. You can wrap them around the pews, pillar and altar for a fairytale look. These are a cheap investment to make and can be used on later occasions.

If you will be using flower arrangements as well, go sparingly on the other decorations.. You may even prefer to make do with just flowers and a few candles.

> **IMPORTANT TIP: MAKE SURE TO USE A NON-SLIP AISLE RUNNER!**

Tips for wedding reception decoration on a budget:

- Complement the color scheme with your flowers and cake, and this should be your styling starting point – and there's no extra cost as those things are already paid for.

- One of the most cost effective ways for coordinating your color scheme is by using chair covers. One of the hottest trends currently is to use two different colored organza sashes across a white chair cover that match the colors of the napkins. Renting chair covers is really worth it and not that expensive

- Light up your special day! Simple lanterns and tea lights can create a wonderful effect with very little money. Color-coordinated paper lanterns can also add an impressive touch of elegance and warmth if you hang them from the ceiling or trees around your venue.

Centerpieces

You could use the bridesmaid's bouquets after the ceremony to decorate the cake table. Delegate the task to one of your bridesmaids to do before the party moves to the reception hall. The cost – zero!

Using a small, hollowed out pumpkin as a flower holder for centerpieces is a creative idea that looks great and doesn't cost much.

You could use dried peas and potpourri to hold centerpiece candles and flowers in place – this also looks great and costs next to nothing

You could also fill vases or pretty glass bowls with water and place flowers or floating candles in them.

Wedding favors

Wedding favors are small gifts given as thank you presents by the bride to her guests. Whereas some brides don't like this idea, others think it's a nice gesture to thank people for attending their special day.

Wedding favors range from the crazily exorbitant; some of the rich and famous have been known to give guests favors ranging from bottles of expensive wine to watches to Tiffany jewelry. Again, my personal opinion is that this is way over the top.

Opinions differ as to whether wedding favors as a must. Some consider it bad manners if you don't give your guests some kind of wedding favor as small souvenir from your wedding. However, this is not carved in stone, and I doubt the lack of wedding favors will seriously offend anyone. They've come to celebrate your wedding and have a good time, not to collect a gift, so if want to forego this step because you just don't have the time or can't afford the extra expense, no problem at all. However, if the idea of expressing thanks to your guests appeals to you, you can do so without breaking the bank.

Tips for choosing budget-friendly favors for your wedding

The following ideas are simple, cheap but also unique. They're sure to put a smile on your guests' faces.

- You could go with the tradition type favor of placing pieces of the wedding cake in pretty transparent boxes decorated with ribbon or flowers.

- Give an ethnic touch to your favors by giving prettily-wrapped small bottle of Sake or a small bunch of Swiss chocolates.

- Make your own favors; you could use homemade candles decorated with ribbons, or beautiful tulle sachets tied with ribbons and filled with potpourri, or even little birdhouses that you could decorate yourself. These make lovely souvenirs as well

- Your favors could also follow the general theme of your wedding. For example, if the wedding is on a beach or the venue is near the beach, little toy boats filled with candy will go over great with your guests. For a winter theme, prettily wrapped dried fruits, a box of snowflake chocolates or soaps, or a snowflake bookmarks.
- If you're having a country wedding, consider miniature potted cacti plants wrapped in cellophane paper tied with strips of rawhide, or cowboy boots magnets.
- For a spring wedding nothing could be more romantic than a spring blossom, to decorate your favors.
- "Practical" wedding favors also go down very well. Little photo albums, bottle stoppers, card holders. A word of warning here: Don't cross the line into tacky with these types of favors. Kick-knacks are fine if they're unique. Key chains and cheap picture frames will not go down well as your guests will feel you did not take the time or effort to put any thought into their gifts.

Reminder: Throughout all these reparations you should be regularly referring to the checklists we're giving away with this book and crossing out that tasks that have been completed. These checklists are available on our website:

http://www.realworldweddingplanning.com

Your wedding favors can either be distributed by the bridesmaids among the guests or placed individually on the tables and used as centerpieces.

Fun Fact: 6 tackiest wedding favors – AVOID AT ALL COSTS!

- Photo key chains,
- Wedding bells
- Cheap picture frames,
- Any kind of noisemaker
- Religious tracts – yes, it has been done!

Wedding make or break – The food

Food can take a huge chunk out of your wedding budget as well as a huge chunk of your time poring over menus, trying to decide what dishes to serve at your reception. The variety of foods is endless, you want to please all your guests while not going overboard on the costs – mission impossible, right? Wrong. Read on for some effective ways to do tall that smoothly and efficiently.

Your wedding banquet

The Mini-feast

As mentioned earlier, you may forego s dinner a full dinner if you're having an afternoon wedding which will usually start after the guests have had lunch. Instead of a full meal, you could serve a variety of rich appetizers or finger foods, which don't have to be too fancy, like small sandwiches, fresh fruits, or cheese and crackers, where you can also choose the less expensive varieties of cheese and cold cuts. Rolls and butter and an assortment of nuts will also be a great addition to this mini feast.

The Brunch Banquet

Another option is to have an earl church wedding and breakfast or brunch right afterwards. This saves so much more money than a full dinner. Follow it with lots of music and dancing and your guests will enjoy themselves thoroughly and talk about what a great time they had for weeks to come! You can serve delicious French toast, bacon and sausages, pancakes, and omelets which are all widely loved and cheap in cost. A brunch will save a lot on alcoholic beverages as well. For drinks you can serve juice or smoothies.

Potluck perhaps?

It's a thought, especially is on the informal side. A potluck wedding is also a great idea – but it depends on how well your friends and family members can cook! Ask guests to bring food instead of a gift. You'll most likely find they'll be pretty enthusiastic about this, each wanting to prepare his or her "specialty dish" for the special occasion. You will have to coordinate with the guests on what each will bring, though. You don't want a table full of desserts and no dinner!

Fresh from the oven

Baking your own desserts is a big money saver. White wedding cupcakes with white frosting or assorted wedding cookies could be much cheaper than fancy – and quite expensive -wedding pastries.

Al Fresco

Another great idea for an outdoor wedding. A barbecue wedding reception with hamburgers, hot dogs, chicken, and grilled veggies, would be great, with side dishes of macaroni salad, buns and potatoes and you're set.

What do drink?

Offering a limited bar that serves soda, water, beer, and wine is guaranteed money-saver.

You could also look for sales on drinks you're planning to serve and stock up before the wedding.

To cut down even more, an alcohol-free wedding reception and serve punch or mocktails instead. This may not go down too well though unless all of your guests are teetotalers. Most guests expect to be served wine or other drinks at a wedding banquet.

Calling Betty Crocker! The Cake

"In all of the wedding cake, hope is the sweetest of plums" - Douglas Jerrold

Your cake is the centerpiece of the reception and the cake-cutting ceremony is the highlight of every wedding. The cake itself has traditionally symbolizes fertility, purity and prosperity. During the cake-cutting ceremony, the custom is the bride cuts the cake while the groom places his hands over hers as she does so. This represents the first joint act as husband and wife!

The cake should be cut from the bottom layer and never at the top. After the bride and groom have had their bites (where custom requires that the bride takes the first bite then the cake goes to the kitchen to be cut, sliced and served to the guests.

The cake should come pretty high up on your list of things to do in the very early stages of planning, ideally 3 to 6 months before the wedding. Once you've decided on your color scheme and booked the venue, you should choose/design/ order the cake leaving this until the "crunch" period, i.e., the last two months is not recommended. In fact, it's one of the cardinal sins of wedding planning as we'll discuss a bit later.

What's in a cake?

Every cake tells a story and your wedding cake tells yours. Choosing the design and flavor of your wedding cake will tell others what you and your groom's share in vision, taste and style.

Whether you're making your own cake or ordering you need a design. I recommend you go no further than the internet for this, A simple image search will allow you to access and endless variety of cake designs.

Take your time – several days if you want and enjoy the task of selecting your ideal cake design. Be creative; you want the cake to be truly memorable not only for the both of you but for your guests as well. Narrow down your choices and finally, select a winner. Decide what flavors you want it to be and any personal touches you want to add. Then If you are ordering your cake, do so right away and cross it off your list.

Note: When planning a wedding cake there are two cardinal sins you must never commit:
1- Waiting till the last minute. If you're ordering a custom-made cake, remember that most bakeries and custom cake shops are usually booked weeks or months in advance. If you plan to make your own cake, also give yourself enough time for trial and error, to experiment with different ingredients and decorations until you get it just right. Trust me, this is not something you want to leave till the last minute.
2- Keep the planning between you and your spouse and perhaps one or two very close friends. Too much input is lie too much yeast – it'll simply ruin the cake. Choosing the cake is about you and your fiancé. Too much output from mothers and friends can drive you crazy with indecision.

Planning a wedding cake on a budget:

Chain store bakery

I have found that many chain store bakeries are truly underestimated. Some of them make the most superb baked goods and desserts – including cakes. Make a round of these bakeries and see what they have to offer. Many will agree to make wedding cakes for very affordable prices.

Local Bakery

Although prices at local bakeries tend to be higher than chain store bakeries, the costs are still much less than elsewhere. Your local bakery can provide a professionally-made elegant cake that looks and tastes great,

Baking class – Cooking school

This is a really creative alternative. Contact a local cooking school or baking class and ask them if they will make your wedding cake. Granted, this may be a bit of a risk but could also be wildly successful. Offer to pay for the materials and leave some time for several attempts. And added bonus is that you get to keep going in for cake tastings!

Wedding cake gift

Ask one of your relatives if they would be willing to "give" you a custom-made cake as an early wedding gift. Or if you have a friend or relative who is good with cakes, offer to pay for the ingredients and ask them to make it.

Make your own

This is another less expensive option but if you are not an experienced baker you may not want to risk it. If you do decide to make your own cake, just make sure that you practice. Make three trial cakes until you're satisfied that everything is just right

Of course, the best money save out of the above is to make the cake yourself or have a friend or relative bake it. Considering the cost of some cake mixes and frostings you can see how baking your own cake can save money.

Extras:

Sometimes nuts and mints are passed out or served with the wedding cake. If your budget allows for this, buy the nuts and make the mints yourself with this scrumptious recipe:

WEDDING CREAM MINTS

Ingredients
1 three-ounce package of softened cream cheese
3 cups powdered sugar
Food coloring (in your wedding colors)
Peppermint Flavoring (available at most grocery stores)

Mix cheese, flavoring, and coloring till well blended. Slowly add sugar. Mix in with fingers as mixture thickens. Roll into small balls then into granulated sugar. Press flat with a spoon. Refrigerate or freeze. Defrost and store in refrigerator 1-2 days prior to serving.

This makes 50-75 mints. Plan on serving 2 mints per person.

To party or not to party? Beverages

For couples who don't want to spend too much money on alcohol, but who would also like to be able to have a classic toast with champagne, one option is to simply just get enough champagne for everybody to have one small glass at the toast, Don't get the champagne out until right before the toast, and serve only one glass to everybody.

Serve a marked drink, such as an alcoholic punch or favorite cocktail instead of providing an open bar.

Many guests will appreciate it if you serve nonalcoholic beverages, such as punch, mineral water, soft drinks, coffee, tea and something sparkling for the toast.

For wine with dinner, figure 2 glasses per person, so at 5 glasses per bottle, for 100 drinking guests you would need 40 bottles.

Music at the reception

Wedding music is the most one of the most important elements of a successful wedding. Music and dancing will make your event more enjoyable for you and your guests so no matter how tight your budget, this is one thing that should be on your list.

The music you choose should be a good mix to suit everybody's taste. Include a variety of songs that your friends will like but don't ignore grandmas, grandpas and older guests. Don't worry, this does not necessarily mean polka music there are loads of oldies that your senior guests will love and that are wonderfully romantic and nostalgic as well.

Tip: The older guests will probably be among the first to leave so choose your music selections accordingly where you can play more 40's and 50's hits mixed with a few modern selections at the beginning of the reception. Keep the more modern stuff for later and let your younger guests cut loose on the dance floor!

Your wedding reception should be fun and exciting throughout, from the entrance of the bride and groom up to the cutting of the cake and dancing afterwards. Music can reflect the theme of your wedding if you have one and you should choose the music just as carefully as you have chosen the theme.

Music on a budget

Music can take a big bite out of your budget, especially if you want live accompaniment during the ceremony and a band for the reception. Music for the wedding reception can be live or recorded performances. If you can afford to hire a band, do so, otherwise a D.J. will be fine. Some wedding venues may include live music as part of the package so you may want to consider that when booking your reception as that may be a cost-saver as well.

If you know someone who can play piano or guitar ask him to play as a gift for you on your wedding day, and if you know someone who can sing and has a good voice let him do this favor for you on your special day.

A local amateur band is another great money-saver. A live band will keep the wedding hopping but who says you have to hire pros? An amateur band will jump at the chance to showcase their talents and get those feet tapping without charging top dollar. Check out your local universities or ask your friends. Just be sure to audition them first.

If you do hire a professional band, reduce the time they are going to play and cut down on costs. You can hire them for an hour just for the dancing and play recorded music for the remaining time of the reception.

Pay attention to the time. Sometimes when the ambience is really rocking, some couples ask the band o keep playing on past the allotted time which can really run up a huge bill.

Many bands offer discounts for non-peak dates as well while charging more for Fridays and Saturdays.

Of course the cheapest method is to play your own music. There are several sites that offer free and completely legal playlists that you can play from a laptop plugged into a surround system with an adaptor wire. Check out mixpod.com and playlist.com for more details.

Miscellaneous

Wedding rings

Wedding rings represent the union of two people joined by the ring finger, which is usually the fourth finger in the left hand in many parts of the world. Why? Because it is believed that the Latin name "vena amoris" or "vein of love" runs directly from the heart to this finger. In other parts of the world such as Germany, Poland, Russia, the ring is worn on the right hand.

The engagement ring components are the diamonds, the metal to choose, and the engagement ring design.

Most wedding and engagement rings are made of Gold or Platinum; gold is cheaper than platinum. 18 kt gold whether it's yellow, white or rose gold is the best choice for rings followed by 14 kt gold.

There are four important things to look for when choosing your ring design:

- It must be simple and comfortable to wear

- It has to look good.

- It has to withstand everyday wear.

- It has to hold its diamonds securely.

Remember the four Cs!

Generally, wedding rings should comprise 3% of your wedding budget, and before buying your wedding ring remind yourself about the "four c's" of diamond quality: Cut, Color, Clarity, and Carat.

Attendants' Gifts

Attendant gifts are little gifts that you buy as a way to express your appreciation to your bridesmaids, groomsmen, ushers, parents, and all the people who helped you to make your dream day a success.

For the youngest attendants such as the flower girl, toys and candy would be great ideas.

For the bridesmaids personalized jewelry such as necklaces, bracelets, earrings, cute framed pictures of all the girls together are great ideas.

For the mother of the bride or the mother of the groom a jewelry box or a compact mirror would be charming.

Groomsmen would enjoy watches, leather goods, or desk accessories.

The Honeymoon

In order to plan for a romantic and cheap honeymoon consider the following points:

-Let the deal be the inspiration! where you can spend a very romantic time with much less cost in Mexico, say, instead of Hawaii, while locations like Buenos Aires will offer the big city cultural experience of Paris but with much less cost.

-Go off season. Going off season doesn't mean the place will be any less beautiful, it only will be much less expensive, for example Europe is the most expensive in the summer, so you should consider going in a month like October which would be much cheaper. Generally, fall is the least expensive time of the year to travel and great discount travel deals are the easiest to find in the fall.

Avoid thanksgiving week and all government holidays because demand is higher and prices are usually hiked up.

Research early, book late. Never book too early like a year in advance of your wedding, this is not considered a good strategy. Instead you can book within a few months before your trip where you can find the best deals. Also, following travel vendors and hotels on face book and twitter could really help.

Tip: Get romantic: Surprise your soul mate during your honeymoon with something special like a shared spa treatment, a romantic dinner on the beach, a sunset cruise.

Top Honeymoon Tip: Be sure to let the hotel know that your reservation is for a honeymoon couple. Many hotels offer special courtesies and gifts for honeymooners and you could get extra special services, offers or discounts, like free champagne, food, or other exclusive treats.

Summing up/General tips

-If your budget doesn't allow you to buy your own wedding dress consider renting one.

- If you're budget allows you to buy your own wedding dress, buy a white dress that is not marketed as a wedding dress, such as a prom dress or regular evening gown. Dresses marketed as wedding dresses are far more expensive than regular white dresses.

-Never mind buying an expensive silk dress, they're more expensive, harder to clean and wrinkle like mad.

-Shop for your wedding shoes off the shelf from regular shoe stores. Avoid bridal shops which will be much more expensive.

- For men, tuxedo rental prices are all pretty much in the same range, you only have to check the condition of the suits and accessories.

-You can pick just one flower from your bridal bouquet to toss instead of tossing the whole bouquet if you want to keep it as a souvenir, and in this case you don't have to bother buying a duplicate bouquet as many brides do.

-Silk flowers save a lot of money; you can use them in your centerpieces, decorations, or altar arrangements.

- Kill two birds with one stone! If you're using bombonieres as guest favors, a good idea is to also use them as centerpieces.

-To make your invitations more personal and much cheaper, do them yourself.

- On buying wedding favors, consider going to a dollar store and checking out the selection they have!

-Buy a plain simple sponge wedding cake or make your own and decorate it yourself using glitter, sugar flowers, or edible pearls which you can buy cheaply from any supermarket.

-Instead of making a big cake you can make three small ones, or even cupcakes.

-Try to hire only one person that does both your hair and makeup do your own or call on the assistance of a friend

-Holding your wedding in a hotel has a lot of good points as they usually decorate, and have professional services and offers like the D.J, offering the honeymoon suite together with discounted rooms for out-of–town guests.

- You don't have to pay a fortune for transportation; you can always rent your cars instead of using a   limousine. Some companies have a large variety of new model luxury cars or sport cars which will be much cheaper, the other members of the party can ride with their husbands, boyfriends, or girlfriends.

-When choosing your music service keep in mind that a D.J is cheaper than a band, and that an amateur band is cheaper than a professional one. The lesser the number of extras (lighting, smoke, fireworks) the cheaper the costs.

-Check the diamonds of your wedding ring carefully, and don't forget to insure your ring.

- You shouldn't borrow to pay for the wedding. Try to avoid that at all costs so that you don't leave yourself in debt at the start of your married life.

-Think carefully about guests, narrow down your guest list, stick only to close friends and family if you're on a tight budget.

Budget tracking sheets and checklists:

When you start to plan for your wedding you will need an easy to use checklist to keep you organized as well as a separate budget sheet to track expenses. The items in this checklist may vary according to your specific needs but we have provided you with three checklists that cover the basics.

We have made a special template available to you for tracking your wedding expenses, so that you know exactly where the money is going. Use the worksheet to document expenses for your wedding as keeping track of everything you spend ensures that you stay within your budget.

Print it out, keep it in your purse, calendar or wedding notebook so that you remember to record entries as soon as you make purchases. Don't leave out anything no matter how trivial you may think it is – it's actually the little costs that may add up to a huge chunk of money.

You may need to customize this worksheet according to your wedding plans.

We've also provided a task checklist. To make your life a whole lot easier. All of these are on our website:

http://www.realworldweddingplanning.com

Conclusion:

"Love is the expansion of two natures in such fashion that each include the other, each is enriched by the other." - Felix Adler

I believe that the getting married is the single most important step that you will ever take in this life.

The quest for love is one of our main purposes in life. As human beings, we can't live without love. When find your soul-mate you realize that you want to spend the rest of your life with that person – you want the rest of your life to start as soon as possible and you want that special day to be a perfect commemoration of your love

Just remember...

Your wedding is all about you and your special other. As long as you're happy on your wedding day, you don't need anything more!

A successful wedding doesn't have to be an expensive wedding, success is marked by whether the bride, groom, and guests enjoyed themselves or not.

Marriage is a holy union although so many people forget that these days. Respect your marriage vows and remember that a marriage is hard work; so put in the effort to keep your marriage happy, romantic, dull of fun – and forever.

Make every wedding anniversary a memorable one; always take plenty of pictures, plan something romantic and watch yourselves grow old together.

And finally, give your heart to the man who truly deserves it. it!

I hope this book will be a helpful guide in planning for your wedding while hopefully enjoying every minute. Yes, it's a huge task for a very special event but with a little bit of planning and creativity, you can make your special day everything you've always dreamed of. **Enjoy the day, don't stress too much, and I wish you a healthy, happy, fabulous, wonderful life together!**

CONGRATULATIONS AND GOOD LUCK!

ABOUT THE AUTHOR

Kristen is an expert at event design; planning, coordinating, and exciting weddings and other social occasions. She is a premier party planner with many high end affairs to her credit. However, her passion is in delivering spectacular results within a tight budget. Kristen lives at home with her cat, two children and amazing husband.